MY LIFE IN THE WILD
PANDA
writer Meredith Costain
illustrator Stuart Jackson-Carter
RED LEMON PRESS

I am a giant panda.

I have thick, fuzzy, black and white fur. My home is the snowy mountains of central China. My name means 'big bear cat'. Let me tell you my story.

I am born with pink skin and soft fur.
I stay with my mum in our den, drinking her milk and resting in her giant paw. For the first few days, Mum never leaves me, even to get food or water.

My eyes have finally opened.
Each day, Mum carries me out
of the den to the forest.

She hides me in a patch of bamboo while she eats. Later, she carries me back to the safety of the den.

Every day I grow bigger and stronger.
I'm learning how to walk, but I fall down a lot.
Mum helps me practise my climbing.

Mum teaches me how to find juicy bamboo shoots.
We sit together on the forest floor, munching happily.

A hungry snow leopard comes sniffing around.
I squeal in terror and hide behind Mum.

Mum growls at the snow leopard.
She stares it down till it slinks away.

The days grow colder and colder. We move further down the mountain where the air is warmer and the streams still flow.

There are lots of tasty shoots to eat here. Mum marks the rocks and trees to keep other pandas away.

The snow is finally melting. We move back up the mountain again.

I'm big enough to climb trees now. I spend most of my day up here, eating and sleeping. Mum is always close by.

Two summers and winters pass. I have learnt everything I need to know from my mother. It's time for me to find my own patch of forest.

Another panda comes to visit me.
He sings to me all day long. I bark a reply.

Soon, a new panda arrives.
My friend charges at him, scaring him away.

I now have a cub of my own. We play together in our patch of forest, rolling and tumbling. Soon I will teach him everything my own mother taught me.

Did You Know?

Baby pandas are tiny.

A newborn panda cub weighs about 85 grams (3 oz) and is about the length of a pencil. The mother is around 900 times the size of her baby! The cub has pink skin and small amounts of fuzzy fur. It cannot see or hear.

Mothers carry young cubs in their mouths, like cats do with kittens.

At around three weeks, the mother takes her cub with her when she goes into the forest to feed. She hides the cub in a patch of bamboo while she eats.

Cubs begin to walk at 3 to 4 months.

For the first three months, pandas can only move by rolling from side to side. They lie on their backs and kick their legs in the air. Their first steps are very wobbly. They also practice their tree-climbing skills, using their mother as a 'climbing frame'.

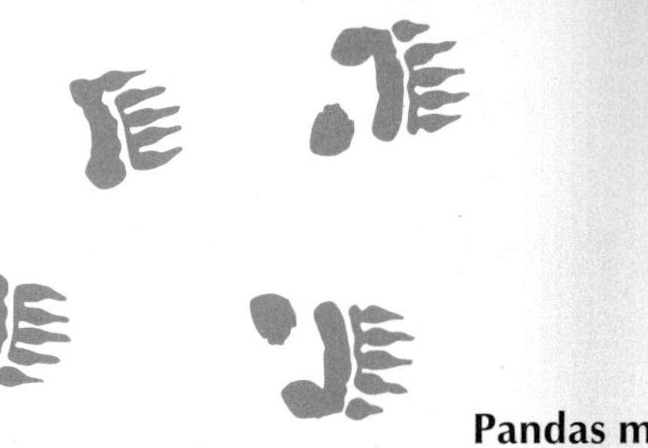

Pandas mainly eat bamboo.

Bamboo makes up 99 per cent of a panda's diet. It is not very nutritious, so pandas need to spend up to 12 hours a day eating to get enough energy to live. On average, each day an adult panda will eat several hundred bamboo stalks, weighing about 12 kilograms (27lb).

Pandas have few predators.

Because of their large size, pandas have few predators. They are able to protect themselves and their cubs against attack with their claws and strong jaws. However, snow leopards, weasels, foxes, wild dogs and martens may eat unguarded cubs.

Unlike other bears, pandas do not hibernate in the winter.

Because bamboo is available all year round, pandas do not need to hoard food, hibernate or travel seasonally to find it. However, they often move down to the lower slopes and valleys where the air is warmer in winter.

Did You Know? (continued)

Pandas scent mark their territory.

Pandas mark their territory by spraying urine or rubbing their anal glands on trees or rocks. Sometimes they perform handstands so they can leave their mark as high up a tree branch as possible. This lets other pandas know to keep away from their food supply.

Cubs spend a lot of their day in trees.

Panda cubs begin to climb trees at around five months. They grip the branches with their sharp claws and haul themselves up. Trees provide a place to play and sleep as well as protection from predators.

Pandas are solitary animals.

Cubs stay with their mother for about two years, learning the skills they will need to survive on their own. After this they leave to find their own home range to live in. The only time they look for other pandas is when they are ready to mate.

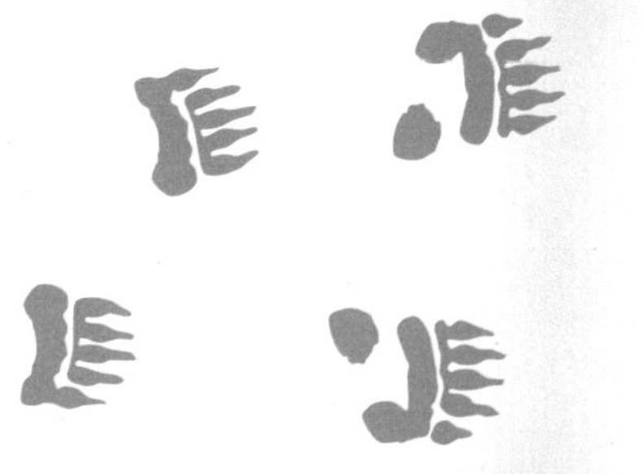

Male pandas compete with each other at mating time.

Male and female pandas come together to mate in the spring. The male then leaves the female to raise the cub on her own. Males may need to travel a long way to find a female panda as their habitat is shrinking.

Female pandas are good mothers.

After giving birth, female pandas hold their cubs almost constantly. They don't leave the birth den to get food or water for themselves till the cub is a week old. Mothers sleep sitting up with their cub in their arms. As it grows older, a mother panda gives her cub lots of cuddles and encouragement.

Meet the Bear Family

Giant pandas are bears. Here are some of their other family members:

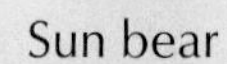

Sun bear

FACT

Pandas are good swimmers.

Grizzly bear

Polar bear

QUIZ

1. Which of these bears is the largest?

2. Which is the smallest?

3. Which bears have black and white fur?

4. Which bear would be hard to spot against snow?

Giant panda

Scientific name: *Ailuropoda melanoleuca*

Coat colour: White with distinctive black patches

Height: Up to 1.5 metres (5 ft)

Weight: Up to 160 kilograms (355 lb)

Life span: 15–20 years in the wild

Diet: 99 per cent bamboo

Habitat: Isolated bamboo forests in the mountains of south-western and central China

Conservation status: Endangered (estimates vary from 1500 to 3000 in the wild)

Giant panda

Red panda

Asiatic black bear

European brown bear

5. Which bears have white markings on their upper chest?

6. Which bear has a stripy tail?

7. Which bear looks the most scary?

A: 1. Polar bear **2.** Red panda **3.** Sun bear, Asiatic black bear, giant panda **4.** Polar bear **5.** Sun bear, Asiatic black bear **6.** Red panda **7.** Grizzly bear!

Glossary

bamboo	a kind of giant grass with tough, hollow, woody stems
charge	to rush at
grasslands	land covered with grass rather than shrubs and trees
den	a cave or tree hollow where a giant panda gives birth then looks after her cub in its first weeks
mark	to leave an odor on a tree or rock to show its territory and warn other pandas to stay away
shoots	the new growth of a plant
snow leopard	a large cat from central Asia with long, thick, white fur
squeal	to make a high-pitched howl
stream	a small river

Published in the UK by:
Red Lemon Press (An imprint of Weldon Owen)
Deepdene Lodge,
Deepdene Avenue,
Dorking,
Surrey RH5 4AT
www.weldonowen.co.uk

Conceived and produced by
Weldon Owen Pty Ltd
Ground Floor 42–44 Victoria Street, McMahons Point
Sydney NSW 2060, Australia
weldonowenpublishing.com

WELDON OWEN PTY LTD

Managing Director Kay Scarlett
Publisher Corinne Roberts
Creative Director Sue Burk
International Sales Laurence Richard
Sales Manager, North America Ellen Towell
Managing Editor Averil Moffat
Senior Editor Barbara McClenahan
Consultant Dr. George McKay
Design Concept Cooling Brown Ltd
Designer Gabrielle Green
Images Manager Trucie Henderson
Production Director Dominic Saraceno
Prepress Controller Tristan Hanks
Illustrations Stuart Jackson Carter
except Meet the Bear Family pages.

ISBN: 978-1-78342-145-9

Printed and bound in China.

A WELDON OWEN PRODUCTION